D1577483

MY FIRST COOK BOOK

David Atherton

illustrated by Rachel Stubbs

WALKER BOOKS
AND SUBSIDIARIES

LONDON • BOSTON • SYDNEY • AUCKLAND

For my dream team: Nik, Kimberley and Mum.
This book is as much them as me.
D.A.

For Rowan, Remy, Poppi, Maisy and Ami – the chefs of our future.
With thanks to Jonathan, for making me laugh and keeping me fed.
R.S.

First published 2020 by Walker Books Ltd, 87 Vauxhall Walk, London SE11 5HJ   10 9 8 7 6 5 4 3 2 1
Text © 2020 Nomadbaker Ltd   Illustrations © 2020 Rachel Stubbs   Additional illustrations © 2020 Walker Books Ltd
"The Great British Bake Off" Baker logo™ is licensed by Love Productions Ltd
The right of David Atherton and Rachel Stubbs to be identified as author and illustrator respectively of this work has been asserted by them in accordance with
the Copyright, Designs and Patents Act 1988   This book has been typeset in Alice and WB Rachel Stubbs   Printed in Italy
All rights reserved. No part of this book may be reproduced, transmitted or stored in an information retrieval system in any form or by any means, graphic,
electronic or mechanical, including photocopying, taping and recording, without prior written permission from the publisher.
British Library Cataloguing in Publication Data: a catalogue record for this book is available from the British Library
ISBN 978-1-4063-9723-9   www.walker.co.uk

All recipes are for informational and/or entertainment purposes only; please check all ingredients carefully if you have any allergies, and if in doubt, consult a
health professional. Adult supervision required for all recipes.

Introduction

I loved my first cook book. I remember taking turns with my twin brother to pick a recipe, and my mum was always on hand to help us. For my family, food wasn't a chore, it was a time to explore and have fun together. It also taught me valuable lessons about creating tasty dishes for other people.

There are so many different ingredients that can be used to make delicious food, and some of these, like fruit and vegetables, are packed with stuff that is good for our bodies as well as our taste buds. I think it's really important to eat healthy food when we can, to make sure we grow strong. You may be surprised to find recipes in this book such as a cake made with avocado, or brownies made with sweet potato, but you'll be even more surprised at how yummy they are.

For me, cooking is all about experimenting with new flavours and recipes, and I want you to feel free to put your own twist on the recipes in this book. Whether it's adding runny honey to slices of cake or jazzing up porridge with fruit or spices, go for flavour combinations your family and friends will love and be as creative as you like! Don't worry if things don't turn out perfectly, they will still taste delicious.

I started cooking when I was very young, and I still get excited about trying out new recipes. I hope you learn something with each dish you create, and that you find recipes which soon become favourites. Recipes that inspire you to tie your apron and dance around the kitchen while creating amazing food!

David

Contents

Starting the day

Purple smoothie glasses 12

Porridge toppers 13

Banana bear pancakes 14

Edible chia bowls 16

Cracking corn bites 18

Scrambled egg surprise! 19

Nutty French toast 20

Breakfast jars 22

Lunches and simple suppers

Magic tomato sauce 24

Soupy tea 25

Snaky breadsticks 26

Piggy buns 28

Tasty tacos 30

The BEST veggie lasagne 32

Happy curry 34

Octo-pizzas 36

Crunchy hedgehogs 38

Perfect pasta bake 40

Easy-peasy pies 42

Veggie hotdogs 44

Satay sticks 46

Delicious treats

Veggie summer rolls 48

Sushi shapes 50

Sweet and spicy dip 52

Hummus lion 53

Fruity jelly jars 54

Banana nut florentines 55

Energy stars 56

Two-tone lollies 57

Ice-no-cream 58

Teatime bakes

Cakey caterpillar 60

Carrot cake 62

Mega-chocolatey cake 64

Sweetie birthday cake 66

Peanut butter bones 68

Honey "Hananah" cake 70

Super-sweet brownies 72

Valentine upside-down cake 74

Victoria sandwich buns 76

Zingy cake squares 78

Heart-stopper scones 80

Golden crumble pots 82

Christmas bauble biscuits 84

A quick kit list

This is the equipment you will use in this book:

Baking paper   Baking tin   Baking tray   Biscuit cutters   Blender

Child's safety knife   Chopping board   Colander   Cooling rack

Frying pan (non-stick)   Grater   Large mixing bowl   Lemon juicer

Measuring jug   Mixer   Muffin tray (12-hole)   Peeler   Rolling pin

Saucepan   Sieve   Spatula   Spoon   Weighing scales   Whisk

A couple of the recipes also use a stick blender or food processor.

Remember to always ask an adult to help!

Cookery words

Beat: use a whisk or spoon to quickly mix the ingredients until they are well combined

Cream: soften the ingredients by mixing them together to make a smooth paste

Cut out: press a biscuit cutter onto the dough, wiggle it a little and release it to make shapes

Dust: use your fingers or a sieve to sprinkle a little flour onto a tray, or icing sugar on top of a bake

Grease: use some baking paper to wipe a little butter or oil on the inner sides of a tin or tray

Knead: give the dough a good bash and stretch it with your hands

Line (a tin): cut some baking paper to the same size as the tin, then press it in

Roll: roll a rolling pin over the dough to make it flatter

Rub: pick up little bits of the mix and rub it through your fingers until all of the mix looks like breadcrumbs

Sift: tap the side of the sieve until the ingredients fall through into a bowl

Spread: use a knife or spatula to move the mix around until it fills a tin or the top of a bake

Weighing and measuring

- All recipes are measured in grams (g) and millilitres (ml)
- Tsp = teaspoon
- Tbsp = tablespoon
- A pinch of something is the amount of an ingredient that you can pick up between your finger and thumb
- The oven temperatures are in degrees centigrade (°C). Increase the temperature by 20°C for a non fan-assisted oven

Before you get going

Before you turn the page, read these handy tips:

- All the recipes in this book will need adult supervision, but it is so good to work together and have fun!

- It takes time to learn how to be safe in the kitchen. Make sure an adult helps you when using a knife, and always wear oven gloves to protect your hands when handling anything hot.

- Some of the recipes use specific baking tins, and even things like lolly moulds or silicone trays. It's a good idea to check you have all the equipment and ingredients needed for a recipe before you start.

- When it says "milk" in this book, the choice is yours. I usually use plant-based milks.

The same goes for vegetable spreads or butters. Make the recipes your own.

- If you have food allergies, or are cooking for someone with food allergies, you need to check the ingredients list carefully.

- Finally, I am a nurse, so it is especially important for me to remind you to wash and dry your hands before you begin cooking, and after handling any raw meat.

Starting the day

Purple smoothie glasses

When I was a kid and I opened a packet of sweets, everyone always wanted the purple ones. This smoothie is for them! The blueberries in this recipe give it the purple colour, but you can also add a handful of red cabbage to make the colour even deeper.

Method

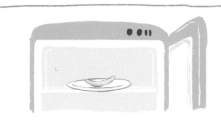

1 Peel the banana and put it in the freezer for at least 3 hours. (I always have bananas in the freezer ready.)

2 Pour the blueberries, honey and milk into a blender and blend.

3 Add the banana and keep blending until completely smooth.

4 Divide between 2 glasses.

Ingredients

1 banana

100g frozen
    blueberries

1 tbsp runny honey

200ml milk

Makes 2 servings

Porridge toppers

I have this breakfast every weekday morning. It warms you up on cold days and gives you energy until lunchtime. I've given you three of my favourite ideas to flavour the porridge, but you can try all kinds of toppings until you find your best one.

Ingredients

500ml milk

100g porridge oats

1 tbsp runny honey

1 tsp tahini

A handful of flaked almonds and extra runny honey to top

Makes 2 portions

Method

1 Put the milk, oats and honey into a saucepan.

2 Warm over a medium heat, stirring continuously with a wooden spoon.

3 When it starts to bubble, keep stirring.

4 Once the porridge is thick, spoon into 2 bowls.

Here are two more ideas from me:

5 Top with a teaspoon of tahini, a squirt of honey and a few flaked almonds.

Add 1 tsp turmeric and 1 tsp cinnamon to the porridge while stirring. Top with a handful of blueberries.

Add a mashed banana to the porridge while stirring, then top with sliced banana when it's in the bowls.

Ingredients

2 very ripe bananas
2 medium eggs
150ml milk
20ml maple syrup
25ml vegetable oil
25g baby spinach leaves
200g plain flour
1 tsp baking powder
Extra bananas,
    blueberries and syrup
    for decoration

Makes 8 pancakes

Banana bear pancakes

These fluffy pancakes taste like bananas, look like cuddly bear faces and are a great green start to the day. Adding spinach to the batter gives them their fun greenish colour and also adds vitamins to the mix. To make the bear faces, I like to add a banana slice for the nose and blueberries for the eyes. Then I pour maple syrup all over the face. Yum!

Method

1 Blend the bananas, eggs, milk, maple syrup, oil and spinach in a blender until very smooth.

2 Put the flour and baking powder in a large bowl.

3 Add the liquid from the blender and mix until combined.

4 Chill in the fridge for 30 minutes.

5 Lightly grease a large frying pan and put over a medium heat. Pour in a circle of batter and then add smaller circles for ears.

6 Allow to cook for 2 minutes, until bubbles cover the surface. Flip and cook for another minute on the other side.

7 Transfer to a plate. Continue until you have a stack of bears.

8 Use a slice of banana for the nose and blueberries for the eyes. Drizzle with a little maple syrup.

Edible chia bowls

This recipe is clever, because you make little bowls that you can also eat! Once you've made your bowls, fill them with whatever you want. I've suggested fruit, yogurt and squiggles of honey, but you could make them even fancier by adding melted chocolate, too.

Ingredients

85g runny honey

25g butter (plus a little extra to grease the tin)

105g porridge oats

25g desiccated coconut

35g chia seeds

1 tsp ground cinnamon

1 large pot of live plain yogurt

Extra blueberries, raspberries and honey for decoration

Makes 12 portions

Method

1 In a small saucepan, melt the honey with the butter over a low heat.

2 Put the oats, coconut, chia seeds and cinnamon into a bowl and mix.

3 Pour in the honey and butter mixture and stir until combined.

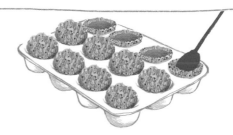

4 Grease a 12-hole muffin tray with a little butter, then put a large spoonful of mix into each hole and press with the back of the spoon to create a dip.

5 Leave this to sit for 1 hour in the fridge and go and play.

6 Preheat oven to 170°C (fan-assisted).

7 Bake for 15 minutes, then leave until fully cooled before gently removing from the tin.

8 Fill with yogurt, then add fruit and a squiggle of honey on top.

Cracking corn bites

When it's cold outside, you want something warm, sweet and soft for breakfast. These are great dipped in your favourite sauce – mine is tomato ketchup. You might want to make double the amount with this recipe, as once you start eating it's hard to stop going back for more!

Ingredients

1 large sweet potato
1 medium carrot
160g tinned sweetcorn
1 medium egg
A pinch of salt
A little vegetable oil

Makes 12 corn bites

Method

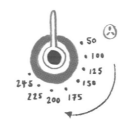

1 Preheat oven to 200°C (fan-assisted).

2 Peel and chop the sweet potato and carrot into chunks. Boil in a saucepan for 10 minutes.

3 Drain and blend until smooth.

4 Tip into a mixing bowl. Add the corn, egg and salt and combine.

5 Grease a 12-hole muffin tin with a little vegetable oil.

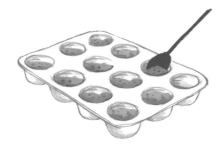

6 Spoon in the mix to half fill each hole.

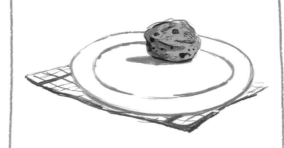

7 Bake for 20 minutes. Allow to cool before eating.

Scrambled egg surprise!

Scrambled eggs are so easy to make – you whisk all the ingredients together and it can't go wrong. These eggs have a surprise ingredient of quinoa to give them a bit more bite, but you can add lots of other ingredients, like chopped veggies or grated cheese, to make them even more special. Once your scrambled egg surprise is ready, spoon it over a piece of hot-buttered toast to serve.

Ingredients

50g quinoa

3 medium eggs

A pinch of table salt

A pinch of baking powder

1 tbsp olive oil

Makes 2 servings

Method

1 Rinse the quinoa, then cook in boiling water – as per cooking instructions – and leave to cool.

2 Whisk the eggs with the salt and baking powder.

3 Drain the cooked quinoa and mix through.

4 Add the olive oil to a frying pan over a medium heat.

5 Pour in the eggs and stir continuously until just cooked, then serve.

Nutty French toast

This is one of my favourite breakfasts – the flavour combo of banana and peanut butter is THE BEST! Stale bread actually works better than fresh bread for this recipe. You'll also need a really good non-stick frying pan as the French toast can get a little sticky.

Ingredients

1 very ripe banana

6 slices of stale bread

A jar of peanut butter

2 medium eggs

75ml milk

1 tbsp runny honey

A little butter to grease
    the pan

Method

Makes 3 sandwiches

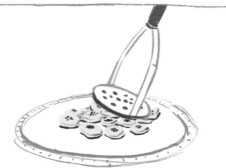

1 Mash the banana on a plate.

2 Spread one slice of bread with one-third of the mashed banana.

3 Spread another slice with some peanut butter and sandwich together. Repeat to make 2 more sandwiches.

4 Whisk the eggs, milk and honey together in a wide-bottomed bowl.

5 Place the first sandwich in the bowl for 30 seconds.

6 Flip it over, leave for 10 seconds and put aside. Repeat steps 5–6 for the other 2 sandwiches.

7 Lightly grease the frying pan and put over a medium heat.

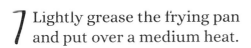

8 Fry the sandwich for 3 minutes. (Don't have the heat too high or it'll burn.)

9 Flip the sandwich over and fry for another 3 minutes. Repeat steps 7–9 for the other 2 sandwiches.

10 Carefully tip each sandwich onto a plate, cut in half and drizzle with honey.

Breakfast jars

If you're up early for a dance class or a sports competition and you need something speedy, this is the perfect go-to breakfast. You prepare it the night before, in jars so you can eat it on the go the next day. You can experiment with the flavours, but cinnamon and honey is my favourite.

Method

1 Mix the oats, chia seeds and cinnamon in a bowl.

2 Grate the apple into the bowl, then add milk, honey and grapes and stir.

3 Divide the mixture equally between 4 jars, screw the lids back on and put in the fridge overnight.

4 To serve you can add yogurt, fruit or any topping you would like.

Ingredients

100g porridge oats

40g chia seeds

1 tsp ground cinnamon

1 Granny Smith apple

250ml milk

1 tsp runny honey

A handful of grapes (chopped in half)

Makes 4 portions

Lunches and simple suppers

Magic tomato sauce

This fresh tomato sauce is made from lots of different vegetables. It's magic because it can be made ahead of time, ready to be used for so many different meals – including several of the recipes in this book. Try adding some to your favourite pasta or veggie noodles. It makes so many meals magic!

Ingredients

2 tins of chopped tomatoes (2 x 400g)

50ml water

1 onion

1 medium carrot

2 sticks of celery

½ a green pepper

5 cloves of garlic

1 tsp table salt

Makes 2 portions

Method

1 Tip both tins of tomatoes into a medium saucepan and add 50ml water. Bring to a simmer over a medium heat.

2 Peel the onion and carrot and roughly chop, along with the celery and pepper, then add to the saucepan.

3 Finely grate the garlic and add this with the salt.

4 Simmer for 30 minutes over a medium heat, then tip into a blender and whizz until smooth. Leave to cool.

5 Divide into 2 portions and keep in the fridge for up to 3 days, or freeze.

Soupy tea

You may have noticed that adults drink a lot of tea! I think you can drink soup like a hot cup of tea, so I pour mine from a teapot and drink it from a mug to make it more fun. You can even serve it at a tea party for your friends and family...

Ingredients

80g split red lentils

2 tsp bouillon powder

1 portion of magic
   tomato sauce

1 tsp ground cumin

2 tsp garam masala

1 tsp ground cinnamon

1 tsp turmeric powder

4 slices of bread

Makes 4 servings

Method

1 Simmer the lentils in a saucepan with 800ml of boiling water and the bouillon powder for 10 minutes.

2 Add the magic tomato sauce and spices, stir and simmer for another 10 minutes over a medium heat.

3 Tip into a blender and blend until smooth. Transfer to a teapot that has a wide spout.

4 Cut the bread into cubes and put in a small bowl.

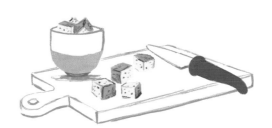

5 Pour the soup into 4 mugs and spoon the bread on top like sugar cubes.

Ingredients

300g plain flour

2 tsp table salt

2 tsp sweet paprika

2 tsp fast-action yeast

1 medium carrot

70ml milk

100ml warm water

Coarse polenta or
   cornmeal and poppy
   seeds to decorate

1 red pepper

16 currants

Makes 8 breadsticks

Snaky breadsticks

I love making bread because you can bash it around with your hands. It can be tricky to roll out, but don't rush, and eventually you'll get a lovely long (and a little scary-looking) snake. Remember that they will rise in the oven, so you need to make them very thin, but you can twist them into any shape you want. I like to make the breadsticks swim in some soup – Soupy tea goes well with this recipe – before I bite the head off.

Method

1 Preheat oven to 160°C (fan-assisted).

2 Put the flour, salt, paprika and yeast in a mixing bowl.

3 Peel and finely grate the carrot.

4 Mix the carrot, milk and water in a jug.

5 Pour the carrot mixture into the bowl and stir until you have a sticky dough.

6 Cover with a damp cloth for 10 minutes.

7 Knead the dough on a floured surface for 5 minutes. (It may be sticky, but don't add any more flour.)

8 Put it back in the bowl and cover with a damp cloth until it has doubled in size. (This may take up to an hour.)

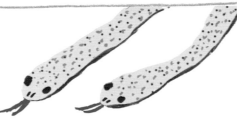

9 Punch all the air out of it and divide into 8 pieces.

10 Dust your worktop with flour and use your hands to roll a piece of dough into a long thin sausage.

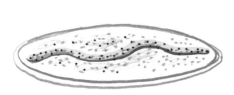

11 Sprinkle some poppy seeds and the polenta onto a plate and then roll your bread snake in it.

12 Choose one end to be the head, cut a little mouth with scissors and add a tongue made from red pepper. Add currants for eyes.

13 Shape the snakes on baking trays lined with baking paper. Leave for 10 minutes and then bake for 8–10 minutes until golden brown.

Piggy buns

These buns are wonderfully soft and are perfect for sandwiches. Once you've baked the piggies, arrange them on a plate to make a pigsty. If you like, you can make other animals, too – I'm going to try a monkey next. What's your favourite animal?

Ingredients

375g strong white
    bread flour
1 tsp fast-action yeast
1 tsp table salt
250ml warm water
A handful of green
    olives to decorate

Makes 12 buns

Method

1 Put the flour, yeast and salt into a mixing bowl.

2 Add the warm water and mix with a spatula until it just comes to a dough.

3 Cover with a damp cloth and leave for 15 minutes.

4 Knead the dough for 15 minutes. It will be quite sticky at the start, but try not to use any extra flour at this stage.

5 Cover again with the damp cloth and leave to rise until it doubles in size.

6 Turn out onto a floured surface, knead for 10 seconds, then divide into 12 pieces.

7 Pull off a small piece for the nose – about the size of a marble – and roll the rest into a ball.

8 Place on a tray lined with baking paper. Roll the nose into a ball and stick on top.

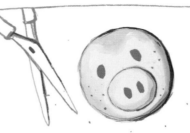

9 Chop an olive into little pieces, then push 2 pieces, hard, into the nose and add 2 pieces for eyes.

10 Once the buns are complete, leave them on baking trays to rise until they double in size.

11 Preheat oven to 200°C (fan-assisted).

12 Use scissors to make 2 snips on top of each bun for the ears, then bakc for 12 minutes.

Ingredients

Tortillas

150g plain flour

50g wholemeal plain flour

30g butter (diced)

120ml water

Taco filling

150g minced beef

1 tsp ground cumin

1 tsp paprika

1 portion of magic tomato
sauce (p. 24)

2 pinches of table salt

1 tin of kidney beans (400g)

Wedges of lime to garnish

Makes 12 tacos

Tasty tacos

It takes time to make your own tortillas, but it's fun and they taste SO nice! If you don't have time, don't worry, it still works with shop-bought tortillas. Either way, you can add lots of toppings to your tacos, like grated cheese, tomato salsa, guacamole or even sour cream, to make them even tastier.

Method

1 Put the flours and a pinch of salt in a bowl and rub in the butter until you have breadcrumbs.

2 Pour in the water and mix to make a dough. (It may be sticky, but don't add any more flour.)

3 Cover the bowl with a damp cloth to keep the dough soft.

4 Leave this to rest for 1 hour.

5 Gently fry the mince over a medium heat until browned.

6 Add the cumin and paprika and fry for another minute. Drain the kidney beans.

7 Add the beans, tomato sauce and a pinch of salt and simmer for 10 minutes, then set aside.

8 Divide the dough into 12 pieces. Take a piece of dough and roll into a ball.

9 Sprinkle a clean surface with flour, then roll out one ball until very thin.

10 Heat a frying pan to a medium-high heat and dry fry for 1 minute on either side.

11 Continue with the rest of the dough, covering the finished tortillas with a clean tea towel.

12 Put a spoonful of the sauce on each tortilla and fold in half.

13 Continue doing this and serve with a wedge of lime.

Ingredients

1 onion

1 tsp olive oil

2 peppers

2 portions of magic
   tomato sauce (p. 24)

1 small sweet potato

A pinch of table salt

1 mozzarella ball

1 bunch of basil

1 box of lasagne sheets

100g cheddar cheese

Makes 6 servings

The BEST veggie lasagne

Lasagne was the first proper meal I made by myself, and
I was so proud! I still love making it today. The fun here
is in the assembly. The best thing about this dinner is
that you can experiment by adding all kinds of different
vegetables in step 2 of the recipe, or you can add some
mince in step 5 to turn it into a meaty dish.

Method

1 Peel and finely chop the
onion. Place in a large frying
pan with a little olive oil and
gently fry for 5 minutes.

2 Dice the peppers, add to
the pan and fry over a
medium heat for a further
10 minutes, until soft.

3 Add the tomato
sauce and stir.

4 Peel the sweet potato
and grate into the pan.

5 Add the salt and
simmer for 15 minutes.

6 Preheat oven to 200°C (fan-assisted).

7 Add one-third of the sauce to a large baking dish.

8 Chop the mozzarella ball into small chunks and add half to the dish with some basil leaves.

9 Place a single layer of lasagne sheets on top.

10 Repeat steps 7–9.

11 Add the rest of the tomato sauce.

12 Grate the cheese and sprinkle on top of the lasagne.

13 Bake for 40 minutes.

Ingredients

1 onion

1 tsp vegetable oil

3 cloves of garlic

A chunk of root ginger (1cm)

1 tsp ground cumin

1 tsp coriander powder

1 tsp turmeric powder

½ tsp ground black pepper

1 tsp table salt

1 tin of chopped tomatoes (400g)

200ml water

300g boneless chicken thighs

200g frozen peas

200g jasmine rice

Makes 4 servings

Happy curry

Take my word for it, curries are so, so tasty, and I'm always really happy when I get to eat this curry! I like to make little smiley faces with some peas before serving it to my friends and family.

Method

1 Peel and finely chop the onion. Add to a large frying pan with the oil and gently fry over a medium heat.

2 Peel and finely grate the garlic and ginger. Add to the pan along with the spices and salt. Fry for 2 minutes.

3 Add the tin of chopped tomatoes and 200ml water and simmer for 15 minutes.

4 Cut the chicken into bite-sized pieces using scissors and add to the sauce.

5 Simmer gently for 10 minutes, then stir and simmer for another 15 minutes.

6 Simmer the peas for 5 minutes in boiling water, then drain and set aside.

7 Put the rice into a small saucepan and cover with boiling water to about 1cm above the rice level.

8 Put over a medium heat. As soon as you see the first bubbles of a simmer, put on a tight-fitting lid and turn down to lowest heat.

9 Leave the rice for 12 minutes and do not remove the lid.

10 Add two-thirds of the peas to the sauce and divide between 4 bowls.

11 Press a quarter of the rice into a ladle – really squash it down – and place in the middle of the curry.

12 Make a smiley face and hair with the extra peas.

Ingredients

375g strong white bread flour

1 tsp fast-action yeast

1 tsp table salt

20ml olive oil

240ml warm water

½ a portion of magic tomato
  sauce (p. 24)

Dried oregano

1 ball of mozzarella

Sliced black olives for
  decorating

Makes 4 pizzas

Octo-pizzas

Making pizza is great because everyone can decide what toppings they want (although I wouldn't suggest a banana!). These pizzas are octopus-shaped. The body is the main pizza and the tentacles are breadsticks – perfect for tearing off and dipping into any leftover magic sauce.

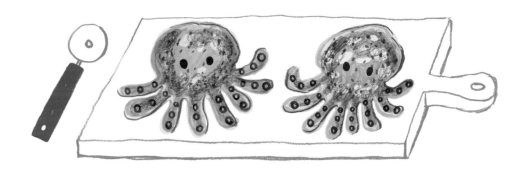

Method

1 Put the flour, yeast and salt into a large mixing bowl.

2 Pour in the oil and water and mix with a spatula to make a dough.

3 Cover with a damp cloth and leave for 5 minutes.

4 Knead the dough in the bowl for 5 minutes. It will be very sticky – but don't worry if it sticks to your hands.

5 Cover and leave in a warm place until it doubles in size. (This may take over an hour.)

6 Preheat oven to 200°C (fan-assisted).

7 Tip the dough onto a floured surface and gently knead until it goes back to its original size.

8 Divide into 4 pieces.

9 Roll out each piece to a circle 0.5cm thick. You can also use your hands to stretch it a little.

10 Transfer each piece to a lined baking tray.

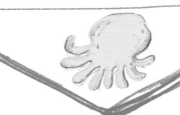

11 Divide the bottom half of the dough into 8. Use your hands to stretch and shape these into legs.

12 Spread the whole thing with the tomato sauce and sprinkle with oregano.

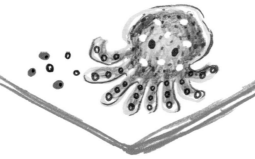

13 Dot the top half with cheese. Place black olive slices for eyes and for suckers along the tentacles.

14 Leave the pizzas to rest for 5 minutes, then bake for 12 minutes until golden.

Ingredients

1 large carrot

500g King Edward
   potatoes

50ml milk

50g cheddar cheese

1 tin of tuna (160g)

50g frozen peas

1 medium egg

100g breadcrumbs
   (panko are
   crunchiest)

Black olives to decorate

Makes 6 hedgehogs

Crunchy hedgehogs

These cute hedgehogs are crispy on the outside and creamy and soft on the inside – and even have a tasty surprise in the centre. If you're feeling adventurous, flavour the mashed potato with a sprinkle of cumin or turmeric to make them even tastier. You can make as many different animal shapes as you like!

Method

1 Peel and chop the carrot and simmer in salted water for 10 minutes.

2 Peel and chop the potatoes.

3 Add to the saucepan and simmer for 10 minutes, until carrots and potatoes are soft, then drain.

4 Mash the potatoes and carrots with 40ml of the milk.

5 Grate half the cheese into the mix and leave to cool for 30 minutes.

6 Preheat oven to 180°C (fan-assisted).

7 Take a handful of the mix and make a ball. Flatten it slightly.

8 Add 1/2 tsp tuna, a few peas and a pinch of grated cheese to the middle. Squash the sides together to make a ball again.

9 Place on a tray lined with baking paper and pinch out the nose.

10 Beat the egg with the rest of the milk.

11 Paint the hedgehogs with the egg mixture and sprinkle with breadcrumbs.

12 Cut the olives into pieces and place as eyes and a nose.

13 Bake for 50 minutes or until golden and crispy.

Ingredients

300g pasta shapes
  (whichever shape
  you like)
2 portions of magic
  tomato sauce (p. 24)
300g broccoli
200g frozen peas
1 bunch of basil
2 tsp dried oregano
A pinch of salt and pepper
100g cheddar cheese

Makes 6 servings

Perfect pasta bake

This is your chance to perfect your own signature pasta bake. Mine has broccoli, peas, basil and oregano in it, but you can choose whatever fillings you want. You can also choose your favourite pasta shape. I like spaghetti because it looks like worms when it's cooked – and it's messy and fun to eat!

Method

1 Boil the pasta as per cooking instructions and drain.

2 Put the tomato sauce into a large bowl and add the cooked pasta.

3 Preheat oven to 200°C (fan-assisted).

4 Chop the broccoli into florets, then simmer for 10 minutes. Drain and add to pasta.

5 Add the frozen peas, tear in the basil, and sprinkle in the oregano and a pinch of salt and pepper.

6 Mix together and transfer to a large baking dish.

7 Grate the cheese and sprinkle on top.

8 Bake for 20 minutes or until the cheese is golden and bubbling on top.

Ingredients

1 medium sweet potato

1 baking potato

50g frozen peas

50g cheddar cheese

1 medium egg

1 tsp table salt

30g tomato paste

1 packet of filo pastry

A little olive oil

Makes 10 pies

Easy-peasy pies

These pies look fancy but they are actually very easy to make. I've used potato, peas and cheese in this recipe, but you can use a mix of any savoury ingredients you'd like. Whichever ingredients you choose, there's nothing better than a hot pie to warm you up on a cold day.

Method

1 Peel and finely grate both potatoes, and grate the cheese. Mix together in a bowl.

2 Add the egg, salt, peas and tomato paste and stir until combined.

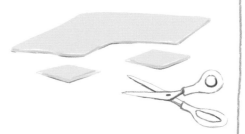

3 Use scissors to cut the filo pastry into quarters (roughly 15cm x 15cm squares).

4 Preheat oven to 180°C (fan-assisted).

5 Brush 10 holes of a muffin tin with a little olive oil. Place a pastry square in one hole, then add 2 more layers.

6 Put a tablespoon of mixture in the middle of the pie and fold the excess pastry over the top. Repeat steps 5 and 6 to make 9 more pies.

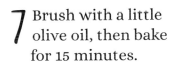**7** Brush with a little olive oil, then bake for 15 minutes.

8 Leave the pies to cool on a cooling rack, then enjoy! Freeze any leftover pies for another day.

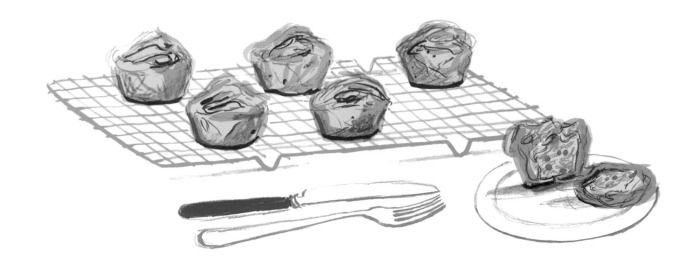

Veggie hotdogs

These cheesy hotdogs can be made for a party, thrown on the BBQ or simply enjoyed as a dinnertime treat. They go nicely inside piggy buns (see page 28) with a good dollop of your favourite sauce to top them off.

Ingredients

1 tin of red kidney
    beans (200g)

80g extra-firm tofu

120g sweet potato

50g cheddar cheese

2 tbsp strong white
    bread flour

A pinch of table salt

1 tsp smoked paprika

1 medium egg

1 tbsp olive oil

6 hotdog buns

Makes 6 hotdogs

Method

1 Drain and rinse the beans, then pour into a food processor and pulse to break them up a bit.

2 Mash the tofu in a bowl with a fork.

3 Peel and finely grate the sweet potato, then add to the bowl.

4 Grate in the cheddar cheese.

5 Add the flour, salt, paprika and egg.

6 Smush with your hands until combined and then chill in the fridge for 30 minutes.

7 Divide into 6 portions, roll roughly then place on a piece of greaseproof paper. Dust with flour and finish rolling to make neat sausages.

8 Chill sausages in the fridge for 1 hour.

9 Pour the olive oil into a frying pan and gently fry for 10–15 minutes, turning with tongs as you go.

10 Add a hotdog to a bun and top with your favourite sauce!

Ingredients

Satay sticks

2 cloves of garlic

A chunk of root
   ginger (1cm)

⅓ tin of coconut milk

2 tsp soy sauce

2 tsp maple syrup

400g extra-firm tofu

Dipping sauce

2 tbsp smooth peanut
   butter

Juice of ½ a lime

1 tbsp soy sauce

1 clove of garlic
   (optional)

3 tbsp coconut milk

Makes 12 servings

Satay sticks

Satay sauce is usually made with peanuts (I LOVE peanuts), but you can do this recipe with other nut butters. I like to eat mine in a toasted pitta bread with a little salad and then dip the whole thing in the nutty dipping sauce.

Method

1 Put the garlic, ginger, coconut milk, soy sauce and maple syrup into a blender and blend until completely smooth.

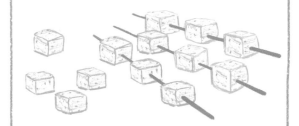

2 Carefully cut the tofu into 3cm cubes. Thread onto 12 skewers.

3 Pour over the marinade and refrigerate for at least 1 hour. Preheat oven to 200°C (fan-assisted).

4 Transfer to 2 lined baking trays and bake for 45 minutes. Leave to cool a little then carefully move the skewers onto a plate.

5 Blend all the dipping sauce ingredients until smooth. You may need to add more coconut milk to get a saucy consistency.

6 Dip in a piece of tofu and enjoy!

Delicious treats

Veggie summer rolls

These refreshing and crunchy rolls are perfect for a summer evening. These are particularly cool because you can see the colourful vegetables from the outside. If you want to make this recipe vegan, just miss out the fish sauce and it will still be super-tasty.

Ingredients

Dipping sauce

3 tbsp smooth peanut butter

2 tbsp lime juice

4 tsp soy sauce

1 clove of garlic (optional)

2 tsp fish sauce

1 tsp runny honey

Rolls

½ an iceberg lettuce

1 medium carrot

½ a cucumber

100g rice noodles

1 packet of 20cm rice paper wrappers

Coriander leaves

Basil leaves

Makes 10 rolls

Method

1 Put all the ingredients for the dipping sauce into a blender and whizz until smooth.

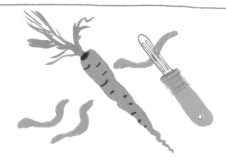

2 Add some water if it's a bit thick.

3 Shred the lettuce into fine strips.

4 Peel the carrot, then keep using the peeler to make ribbons.

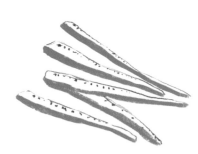

5 Slice the cucumber into thin sticks.

6 Put the rice noodles into a bowl and soak in boiling water for 10 minutes.

7 Drain and set aside.

8 Put a rice wrapper into a bowl of warm water for 15 seconds. Take out and dry on a tea towel.

9 Move wrapper to a damp chopping board. Place noodles, lettuce, carrot strips, cucumber sticks, coriander and basil leaves in the middle and start to roll up.

10 Roll halfway, then fold in the ends and finish rolling. Continue with the rest of the rice wrappers. Serve with the peanut dipping sauce.

Ingredients

200g sushi rice

260ml cold water

80ml rice vinegar

20g caster sugar

A pinch of table salt

3–4 sheets of nori seaweed

½ a cucumber

A handful of sesame seeds

A little soy sauce

Makes 10 rolls

Sushi shapes

Making sushi is a sticky business, but lots of fun. You can use any shaped biscuit cutter you like for this recipe – the more sushi shapes, the better! I like to decorate the sushi shapes with cucumber and sesame seeds, but you can use any crunchy veggies, before dipping it all in soy sauce.

Method

1 Rinse the sushi rice in a sieve until water runs clear.

2 Soak in cold water for 15 minutes, then drain.

3 Put the rice in a saucepan with the 260ml water and bring to a simmer. Put on a tight-fitting lid and turn down to lowest heat.

4 Leave for 15 minutes without removing lid.

5 Take off the heat and leave for another 10 minutes without removing lid.

6 Mix the vinegar, sugar and salt until the sugar and salt have dissolved.

7 Pour over the rice and stir though.

8 Leave to cool and go and play!

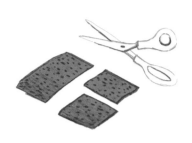

9 Cut the nori seaweed into squares just bigger than your biscuit cutter.

10 Rub some water onto a chopping board. Tip out the sushi rice and press down with wet hands until it is about 1cm in thickness.

11 Dip the biscuit cutter in water and cut shapes out of the rice.

12 Place a rice shape on top of each seaweed square.

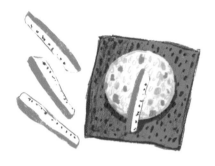

13 Slice the cucumber into sticks and place on top.

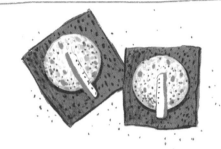

14 Sprinkle with sesame seeds and serve drizzled with a little soy sauce.

Ingredients

1 large sweet potato
1 clove of garlic
3 tsp light tahini
1 tsp table salt
½ tsp smoked paprika
½ tsp ground cumin
Juice of ½ a lime

Serves 4

Sweet and spicy dip

This is one of my favourite go-to treats. It's delicious on its own, and it can be eaten hot or cold. I like to dip pitta bread into it, or spread a lovely thick layer on some toast and sprinkle with seeds.

Method

1 Bake the sweet potato for 45 minutes at 200°C, then allow to cool. (You can do this ahead of time.)

2 Scoop out the sweet potato flesh and put in a bowl. Mash with a fork.

3 Finely grate or crush the garlic and add to the bowl.

4 Add the tahini, salt, paprika, cumin and lime juice and mix together with a fork.

5 Serve with toasted pitta breads.

Hummus lion

Making hummus is so easy. It's super-quick to whizz all the ingredients together and it's so tasty! I like to decorate the hummus with chopped olives to make a fun lion face, and to make a carrot stick mane that everyone can use to dip into the tasty hummus.

Ingredients

4–5 carrots
1 tin of chickpeas (400g)
1 clove of garlic
1 tsp table salt
20ml olive oil
3 tsp light tahini
Juice of ½ a lemon
Black olives to decorate

Serves 4

Method

1 Peel the carrots and carefully slice into carrot sticks.

2 Drain the chickpeas and save 50ml of the water from the tin.

3 Crush the garlic and mix with the salt, olive oil and tahini.

4 In a food processor, blitz the chickpeas with the chickpea water and lemon juice.

5 Add half the oil mixture and blitz again. Then add the second half and blitz until smooth.

6 Put the hummus in the middle of a plate and arrange the carrot sticks around it. Chop the olives into little pieces and use them to make the face.

Fruity jelly jars

This recipe is all about using your favourite fruity flavours. You can choose any fruit juice and add whatever fruit pieces you like. You can even make layers of different colour jellies, just let each layer set in the fridge before adding the next.

Ingredients

500ml fruit juice

1 tsp agar powder

A selection of fruit

Makes 3 jars

Method

1 Pour the fruit juice into a small saucepan and sprinkle on the agar powder. Leave for 5 minutes.

2 Prepare your fruit by chopping it into any shapes you please. You could even use mini biscuit cutters.

3 Slowly bring the fruit juice to a simmer over a medium heat while stirring.

4 Once all the agar powder has dissolved, pour into the clean jars, filling them halfway.

5 Add half of your fruit pieces.

6 Leave until cool, then add the rest of the fruit pieces.

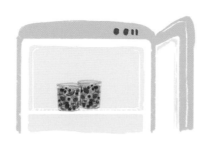

7 Chill in the fridge for 1 hour.

8 Top with extra fruit if you wish.

Ingredients

30g banana chips
1 medium egg white
50g icing sugar
80g flaked almonds
30g raisins
1 tbsp poppy seeds

Makes 12 biscuits

Banana nut florentines

These are sweet, chewy and crunchy – all the best things!
If possible, use silicone mats for this recipe as the florentines
will be so, so sticky and it's very hard to
get them off baking paper.

Method

1 Preheat oven to 160°C (fan-assisted).

2 Line 2 baking trays with silicone mats.

3 Blitz the banana chips into small pieces using a food processor. (Or you can put the chips into a little bag and bash with a rolling pin.)

4 Separate the egg white from the yolk through your fingers (you'll need two people for this).

5 Mix the egg white with the icing sugar, whizzed banana chips, almonds and raisins.

6 Spoon a tablespoon full of mixture onto a silicone mat and press down flat.

7 Continue until all the mixture is used, then sprinkle with poppy seeds.

8 Bake for 10 minutes or until golden. If pale, keep in the oven for another 2–3 minutes.

9 Once out of the oven, allow to cool completely before peeling off the mat.

Ingredients

100g porridge oats

50g dark chocolate

70g dates

70g prunes

Sunflower seeds
    to decorate

Makes 8–10 biscuits

Energy stars

These snacks are full of natural energy and are especially good to eat before you do any exercise, like star jumps! What's more, they're super-quick to make as you don't have to bake them. Don't worry if you don't have a star-shaped cutter, you can use any cutter – they'll taste just as yummy.

Method

1 Blitz the oats in a food processor for 10 seconds and set aside.

2 Melt the chocolate in a jug in the microwave, checking every 10 seconds, until just melted.

3 Blitz the dates and prunes until you have a smooth paste.

4 Pour in the melted chocolate and blitz again until very smooth and shiny.

5 Transfer to a bowl and knead in the oats.

6 Roll out to roughly 1cm thick and cut out with a star-shaped biscuit cutter.

7 Finally, add sunflower seeds on top for decoration.

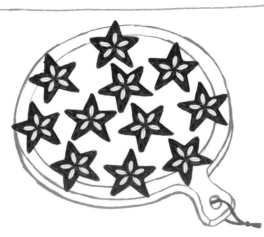

Ingredients

2 bananas

8 grapes (chopped in half)

10 strawberries

Makes 4 lollies

Two-tone lollies

You will always want some of these cool and colourful lollies in the freezer after you've been playing outside on a hot, sunny day. You'll need a lolly mould for this recipe, to make sure the lollies hold their shape and are ready to eat when you're ready to be cooled down.

Method

1 Put 1 banana into a jug or beaker and whizz with a stick blender until smooth.

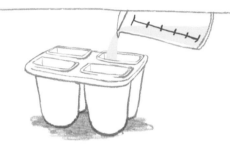

2 Pour into a lolly mould to fill halfway. Push in 2 grape halves and freeze for 1 hour.

3 Whizz the second banana and the strawberries with a stick blender until smooth.

4 Fill up the lolly moulds and push in 2 more grapes.

5 Add the lolly holders and place in the freezer for at least 3 hours.

6 Once frozen, take out of the freezer and run under some warm water to release the lollies.

Ingredients

2 overripe bananas
50g Greek yogurt
2 tsp cocoa powder
1 tsp vanilla extract

Makes 2 servings

Ice-no-cream

Here is an easy way to make your own chocolate banana ice cream, and it's a good way to use up any overripe bananas. It takes time to freeze the bananas, but I promise that it's worth it!

Method

1 Peel and slice the bananas, lay onto small baking sheets and freeze for at least 3 hours.

2 Once frozen, put into a jug or beaker with the Greek yogurt, cocoa powder and vanilla extract.

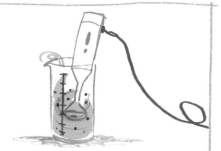

3 Blitz with a stick blender until it has a smooth ice-cream consistency.

4 Quickly divide into 2 bowls and eat!

Teatime bakes

Ingredients

1 medium egg

60ml vegetable oil

45g caster sugar

50g spinach leaves

½ a ripe banana

½ tsp vanilla extract

75g courgette

150g plain flour

1 tsp baking
   powder

65g icing sugar

15ml water

Lots of sweets to
   decorate

Makes 12 cupcakes

Cakey caterpillar

This is my favourite birthday cake – I've had it for five different birthdays so far! I think the best way to decorate it is to put sweets onto cocktail sticks and stand two sweetie sticks up on each cake to make a very furry caterpillar. If you want to make the caterpillar even longer, just double the ingredients!

Method

1 Preheat oven to 180°C (fan-assisted).

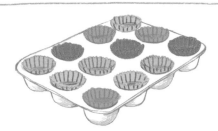

2 Prepare a 12-hole muffin tin with paper cases.

3 In a blender, blend the eggs, oil, sugar, spinach, banana and vanilla until smooth and green.

4 Finely grate the courgette.

5 Mix the flour with the baking powder in a large bowl.

6 Stir in the courgette.

7 Add the blended ingredients and mix until combined.

8 Divide into paper cases (no more than two-thirds full).

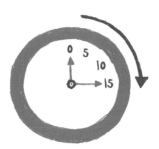

9 Bake for 15 minutes, or until golden, then leave to cool on a cooling rack.

10 Put the icing sugar in a clean bowl, add 15ml of water and mix.

11 Once the cakes have cooled, top with the icing.

12 Arrange in a long wriggly line and decorate with sweets.

Carrot cake

Carrot cake is moist and packed full of flavour. It's a little tricky to grate the carrots, but once you've made this cake I bet you'll want to bake it again and again. If you are making it for a special occasion, use a fork to make a swirly pattern in the icing and then sprinkle it all over with a pinch of cinnamon.

Ingredients

Cake

100g caster sugar

100g soft brown sugar

150ml vegetable oil

3 medium eggs

160g carrots

170g plain flour

2 tsp baking powder

1 tsp ground cinnamon

Icing

150g Greek yogurt

80g icing sugar

1 tsp vanilla extract

A pinch of cinnamon
    to decorate

Makes 12 servings

Method

1 Preheat oven to 160°C (fan-assisted).

2 Grease and dust 2 (20cm) round tins with flour.

3 Beat the caster sugar, brown sugar, oil and eggs until smooth.

4 Peel and finely grate the carrots – or whizz them in a food processor – and add to the bowl.

5 Mix in the flour, baking powder and cinnamon.

6 Divide the mixture between the 2 tins and smooth the tops.

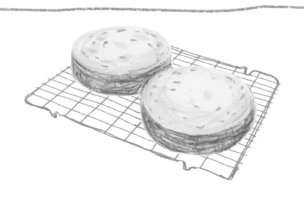

7 Bake for 25 minutes. Turn out onto a cooling rack and leave until completely cooled.

8 Put the yogurt, icing sugar and vanilla extract into a clean bowl and stir gently until just mixed.

9 Spread half the icing on one cake, then make a sandwich with the second cake. Decorate the top with the rest of the icing and a sprinkle of cinnamon.

Ingredients

Cake

260g plain flour

400g caster sugar

25g cocoa powder

2 tsp baking powder

130ml milk

110ml vegetable oil

2 medium eggs

2 tsp vanilla extract

230ml water

Icing

100g caster sugar

40g cocoa powder

30g cornflour

120ml water

1 tsp vanilla extract

20g butter

Makes 24 servings

Mega-chocolatey cake

This cake is mega-easy to make and it always come out so soft and SO chocolatey. The icing is sticky and fudgy, and once it's spread over the cake, you can zhuzh it up by sprinkling even more grated chocolate on top.

Method

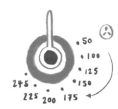

1 Preheat oven to 160°C (fan-assisted).

2 Grease and dust a traybake tin (25cm x 20cm) with flour.

3 Mix the flour, sugar, cocoa powder and baking powder together in a bowl.

4 In a separate bowl, beat the milk, oil, eggs, vanilla and 230ml water.

5 Pour this into the flour mix and beat until smooth.

6 Pour into the traybake tin.

7 Bake for 35–40 minutes, then leave to cool in the tin.

8 In a saucepan, mix the sugar, cocoa, cornflour, water, vanilla and butter over a medium heat, stirring continuously until smooth. If lumpy, transfer to a blender and whizz until smooth.

9 Pour the icing over the cake, and serve slices from the tin.

Sweetie birthday cake

Everyone wants a special cake for their birthday. This cake is a simple vanilla cake, but what could be more special than topping it with spoonfuls of creamy icing and as many of your favourite sweets as you can fit on the cake? It's party time!

Ingredients

Cake

2 ripe avocados

250g caster sugar

4 medium eggs

2 tsp vanilla extract

250g self-raising flour

½ tsp baking powder

Icing

75g soft unsalted butter

225g icing sugar

80g Greek yogurt

1 tsp vanilla extract

Your favourite sweets

Makes 12 servings

Method

1 Preheat oven to 160°C (fan-assisted).

2 Grease and dust 2 (20cm) round tins with flour.

3 Carefully remove the stones from the avocados, scoop the flesh into a bowl and add sugar. Use a whisk to mix until smooth.

4 Beat in the eggs one at a time, then the vanilla.

5 Stir the flour and baking powder into the mix.

6 Divide into the 2 tins and smooth the tops.

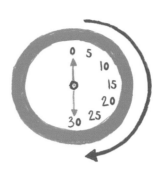

7 Bake for 30 minutes.

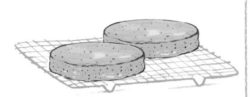

8 Turn out onto a cooling rack and leave until cooled.

9 Beat together the butter and half of the icing sugar until smooth.

10 Add the Greek yogurt, vanilla and the rest of the icing sugar, and whisk together until combined.

11 Spread half the icing on one cake, sandwich the two cakes together and spread the rest of the icing on top.

12 Finish by topping with plenty of your favourite sweets.

Ingredients

280g plain flour

100g caster sugar

A pinch of baking powder

50g unsalted butter (diced)

A jar of smooth peanut butter

1 medium egg

Makes 18 biscuits

Peanut butter bones

I love dogs, and when I was a kid I used to pretend I *was* a dog. These biscuits are for anyone who wants to have fun eating bone-shaped biscuits, just like our furry friends! If you don't have a bone-shaped cutter, don't worry, any cutter will work – just use plenty of peanut butter to sandwich the biscuits together.

Method

1 Combine the flour, sugar and baking powder in a large mixing bowl.

2 Rub in the butter, then add 50g of peanut butter. Continue until the mixture resembles breadcrumbs.

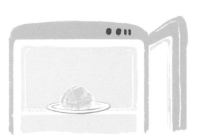

3 Add the egg and bring together to make a dough.

4 Wrap and put in the fridge for 1 hour while you go and play (or tidy your room).

5 Roll out the dough on a floured surface until roughly 0.5cm thick.

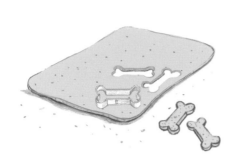

6 Cut out the biscuits using a bone biscuit cutter.

7 Place on baking trays lined with baking paper and chill in the fridge for 30 minutes.

8 Preheat oven to 160°C (fan-assisted).

9 Bake for 10–15 minutes or until just brown.

10 Transfer to a cooling rack.

11 Once cool, sandwich together pairs of biscuits with peanut butter.

Ingredients

100g soft butter

3 ripe bananas

50g honey

80g soft brown sugar

90ml light olive oil

2 medium eggs

80g plain flour

50g wholemeal plain flour

2 tsp baking powder

Extra honey for topping

Makes 8–10 slices

Honey "Hananah" cake

This is my friend Hannah's favourite cake! We often make it together and then eat it together, so I like to think of it as honey "Hananah" cake. This is quite a deep cake, so if you're not sure if it's cooked all the way through, just pop a skewer through the middle. If it comes out clean, the cake should be cooked. After a few days it's best toasted with a little honey drizzled over the top.

Method

1 Preheat oven to 160°C (fan-assisted).

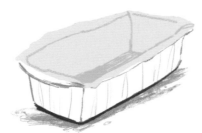

2 Push baking paper into a 20cm loaf tin, then rub with butter.

3 Peel the 2 ripest bananas and put into a food bag. Bash with your hands until mashed thoroughly.

4 Empty the mashed banana into a large bowl and mix with the honey, sugar, oil and eggs.

5 Stir in the flours and baking powder.

6 Transfer mixture to the lined tin.

7 Peel and slice the third banana and place gently on top.

8 Bake for 60 minutes. Use a skewer to test that it's cooked through, then transfer the cake to a cooling rack.

9 Once cool, slice into pieces and drizzle with extra honey.

Super-sweet brownies

If you like chocolate these brownies are for you. They are super-gooey and rich and soft, and the sweet potato adds an extra layer of texture and sweetness. You can use dark or milk chocolate for this recipe and can also add lots of extras such as dried fruit, chocolate chunks or chopped nuts.

Ingredients

1 large sweet potato
90g butter
120g chocolate
120g caster sugar
2 medium eggs
1 tsp vanilla extract
100g plain flour
1 tbsp cocoa powder
½ tsp baking powder
A pinch of table salt

Makes 9 brownies

Method

1 Preheat oven to 200°C (fan-assisted). Bake the sweet potato for 45 minutes, then allow to cool. (You can do this ahead of time.)

2 Scoop out the sweet potato flesh and mash in a bowl until smooth. (You can use a fork or stick blender to do this.)

3 Line a 20cm square tin with baking paper.

4 Turn oven down to 160°C.

5 Melt the butter in a saucepan over a low heat. Break the chocolate into pieces and add to the saucepan, stirring continuously until smooth.

6 Pour the chocolate mix over the sweet potato. Add the sugar, eggs and vanilla and mix together.

7 Add the flour, cocoa, baking powder and salt and mix until smooth.

8 Pour into tin and bake for 30 minutes.

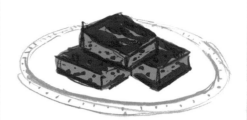

9 Carefully remove from tin and cool on a cooling rack, then cut into 9 squares.

Valentine upside-down cake

Ingredients

1 tin of sliced peaches
A handful of frozen
    raspberries
100g soft butter
150g soft brown sugar
2 tbsp runny honey
1 tsp vanilla extract
1 large egg
150g plain live yogurt
175g plain flour
2 tsp baking powder
Extra runny honey
    to top

Makes 8–10 slices

Let your friends and family know that you love them by giving them a big slice of Valentine upside-down cake and a hug! This cake is fun to make because you don't know what it will look like until you turn it over after baking to reveal the pattern on top. You can use different fruits and make whatever design you like – feel free to experiment!

Method

1 Preheat oven to 180°C (fan-assisted).

2 Push baking paper into a 20cm loaf tin, then rub with butter.

3 Arrange the peach slices and raspberries on the baking paper in your heart design.

4 In a large bowl, beat the butter, sugar, honey and vanilla until smooth.

5 Beat in the egg and yogurt. Gently mix in the plain flour and baking powder until smooth.

6 Carefully spoon the mixture on top of the fruit in the tin. Bake for 40–45 minutes, or until a skewer through the middle comes out clean.

7 Once baked, wait for 10 minutes and then turn the cake over with a plate. Now you can drizzle it all over with honey.

Ingredients

125g soft unsalted
   butter
130g caster sugar
3 medium eggs
160g plain flour
2 tsp vanilla extract
1 tsp baking powder
150g raspberry jam
Icing sugar to dust

Makes 12 buns

Victoria sandwich buns

Sometimes the classics are the best. People have been baking this cake for many, many years, and I'm sure the adults in your life LOVE a Victoria sandwich cake. Surprise them with these mini versions that are baked with jam in the middle.

Method

1 Preheat oven to 180°C (fan-assisted).	*2* Line a 12-hole muffin tin with muffin cases.	*3* Cream together the butter and sugar until pale. 
4 Beat in 1 egg. 	*5* Stir in half the flour. 	*6* Beat in another egg. 

7 Stir in the other half of the flour and the baking powder.

8 Finally, beat in the third egg and the vanilla extract until smooth.

9 Put a dessert spoon of mixture into each case, add half a teaspoon of jam, then put another dessert spoon of mixture over the top.

10 Bake for 20 minutes. Leave to cool, then dust with icing sugar.

Zingy cake squares

Lemons are sour, but when they're used in a mix with a little sugar they can make a sweet and zingy cake. Zesting lemons can be tricky, so if you want to miss this out you can use a few drops of lemon oil instead.

Ingredients

Cake

2 lemons

400g caster sugar

100g soft unsalted butter

130ml vegetable oil

3 medium eggs

300g plain flour

2 tsp baking powder

30g chia seeds

Icing

30g chia seeds

Juice from 2 lemons above

130g unsalted cashew nuts

1 very ripe mango

30g icing sugar

Makes 16 squares

Method

1 Soak the cashews in hot water and set aside to cool. Preheat oven to 160°C (fan-assisted).

2 Grease and dust a square 20cm tin with a little flour.

3 Zest the lemons with a fine grater, then save the lemons for the icing.

4 Beat the sugar, butter, oil and zest until light and fluffy. (You will need to use a mixer.)

5 Add the eggs one at a time and beat in.

6 Beat the flour, baking powder and chia seeds into the mix.

7 Add the mix to the tin and smooth the top.

8 Bake for 40 minutes.

9 Allow to cool in the tin for 10 minutes, then turn out onto a cooling rack.

10 Juice the lemons and pour into a blender. Drain the cashew nuts.

11 Peel the mango and chop it into chunks, carefully removing the stone, then add the pieces to the blender.

12 Add the icing sugar and cashew nuts and blend until smooth. Then finally add the chia seeds.

13 Spread the icing on the cake once cooled. Cut the cake into squares.

Ingredients

350g self-raising flour

1 tsp baking powder

50g caster sugar

85g butter (diced)

170ml milk

Some extra milk

A jar of strawberry jam

Makes 18 scones

Heart-stopper scones

These silky scones look stylish and yet they're so easy to make. The red jam is perfect for the hearts, and the scones are baked with the jam already in, so they're ready to eat as they are. If you want your family and friends to feel even *more* loved, serve with a blob of natural yogurt and a strawberry, then dust with a little icing sugar. Divine!

Method

1 Preheat oven to 180°C (fan-assisted).

2 In a bowl, rub the butter, flour, baking powder and sugar until you have breadcrumbs.

3 Pour in the milk.

4 Mix until it just forms a dough and let it sit for 10 minutes.

5 On a floured surface, roll out the dough until roughly 1cm thick.

6 Cut out scones using a 4cm biscuit cutter.

7 In half of the scones, cut out a heart using a small heart-shaped biscuit cutter.

8 Brush a little milk onto each scone. Place a heart scone on top of each complete scone and fill the hole with jam (not quite to the top).

9 Transfer to a lined baking tray and bake for 15 minutes.

10 Leave to cool on a cooling rack before eating. (The jam will be very, very hot.)

Ingredients

2 Bramley apples

4 tbsp water

1 tsp ground cinnamon

A handful of frozen
    raspberries

30g plain flour

20g wholemeal plain flour

10g ground almonds

40g butter (diced)

40g soft brown sugar

30g porridge oats

Makes 4 pots

Golden crumble pots

My no. 1 favourite dessert! As a kid I loved climbing trees
to collect the apples for making a crumble. I like these puds
as I can have one all to myself with some custard, ice cream
or natural yogurt. What will you have with yours?

Method

1 Peel and core the apples,
then cut into small cubes.

2 Add the apple and
cinnamon to a saucepan
with 4 tbsp water.

3 Gently heat on the lowest
heat for 15 minutes, until
the apple is just starting
to get soft at the edges.

4 Spoon the apple and
frozen raspberries into
4 oven-proof ramekins.

5 Preheat oven to
200°C (fan-assisted.)

6 Put the flours, ground almonds and butter in a bowl and rub until you have breadcrumbs.

7 Add the sugar and oats and rub these through.

8 Sprinkle a little of the mix on top of each crumble until it is all used.

9 Bake for 25 minutes, until golden on top.

Christmas bauble biscuits

These baubles are the best kind of decoration – they make your Christmas tree look so beautiful *and* you can eat them! You can decorate the biscuits as you wish, and can even colour the icing. I like to use a cocktail stick to marble a little coloured icing over the white icing. Just be careful not to eat them all before Christmas Day arrives!

Ingredients

Biscuits

75g butter

1 tbsp honey

50g soft brown sugar

½ tsp orange extract

80g plain flour

50g bread flour

A pinch of baking powder

2 tsp ground mixed spice

½ tsp ground cinnamon

1 small egg

Royal icing

1 egg white

220g icing sugar

1 tsp lemon juice

Makes 20–24 biscuits

Method

1 Melt the butter, honey, sugar and orange extract, then set aside to cool slightly.

2 Combine the flours, baking powder and spices in a mixing bowl.

3 Once the wet mixture is cooled, lightly whisk in the egg.

4 Stir this into the flour mixture. (It will seem very wet.)

5 Pour into a bag and seal. Chill in the fridge until a firm dough.

6 Roll out to roughly 0.5cm thickness and cut out with a 5cm biscuit cutter. Use the end of a pen top to make a little hole in the top of each biscuit.

7 Put on lined baking trays and then chill in the fridge for 30 minutes.

8 Preheat oven to 170°C (fan-assisted).

9 Bake each tray of biscuits for 12 minutes. Allow to cool before removing from tray.

10 Whisk all the icing ingredients together until the icing is thick enough to leave a line on the surface of the mixture for 10 seconds when the whisk is lifted.

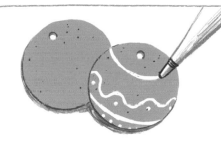

11 Scoop into a piping bag and pipe onto each biscuit. You can add edible decorations on top if you wish.

12 Allow icing to dry until hard before threading the ribbon and hanging on the tree.

Photograph © 2020 Rachel Stubbs

David Atherton is the winner of *The Great British Bake Off* 2019. Before applying to be a contestant on the show, David worked as an international health advisor, spending time in UK Aid-funded hospitals overseas. As well as being passionate about cooking, David is a fitness enthusiast and is always looking for another craft to master. *My First Cook Book* is David's first book for children, with a focus on fun, healthy and imaginative recipes that are sure to inspire the youngest of readers to get cooking.

Rachel Stubbs is a London-based illustrator who loves observing human behaviour and interaction. Having studied illustration in Falmouth, she later joined the Cambridge MA in Children's Book Illustration to refresh her creative practice. Here she rediscovered the joy of drawing from life in her sketchbook, and she loves nothing more than getting outside to draw in her local parks, cafes and museums. Rachel was awarded the Sebastian Walker Award for Illustration in 2017 and her debut picture book, *My Red Hat,* was published in 2020.